THE CREATION OF BIRDS
AND OTHER POEMS

Ameriah Schober

www.ameriah.com

The Creation of Birds and Other Poems

Copyright © 2017 by Ameriah Schober

Cover art: detail from *A Siren and a Centaur*, artist unknown, France, circa 1270

ISBN 978-0-692-88653-3

www.ameriah.com

ONE

The rain sprinkled the rooftop,
And I had known you'd been thinking of me.
Not like when we were together,
Yet just a foggy memory,
Like remembering your second cousin or trying
    a food for the first time.
The faint and serene battering against the
    window
Mimicked the lachryma that caused myself
    when memorializing you.
The rain pelted the rooftop,
And I had known that you hadn't been thinking
    of me.
I was just the fool,
The fool who'd mistaken the torrent for sunshine,
The fool who'd mistaken respect for affection.
For when the rain leaves,
And your thoughts of me disappear,
I will still be within reach.

TWO

Your words envelop my thoughts.
Tangled around my brain,
Circulating my mind,
Until the dizziness makes me weak.
The numbness inside is bearable,
Yet insufferable.
I start to reconsider my actions—
Every single one.
Your fatal tongue slips beneath my ear,
The turpentine pulses venom into my veins,
Until I inhale the poison that you shove down my throat.
The paralysis is surreal,
Yet authentic.
I start to rearrange my delusions—
Every single one.

THREE

I'm still waiting to snap awake from this dream.
Wake up,
Wake up.

FOUR

It's weird how much things change over time.
Your friends today weren't your friends
    yesterday,
Your thoughts today weren't your thoughts
    yesterday.
Another day, another month, another year—
Passes.
And you can't even remember why you're crying.
Or, you do,
But you can't even wrap your mind around why
    you're still hung up on this old memory,
Because it happened years ago—
Months ago—
Days ago.
It's as if nothing is real anymore.
Because you can't believe how things have
    changed—
So fast.
Maybe it isn't real.
Maybe it's just a terrible dream
Or just a splendid nightmare.

FIVE

People always ask me why I am so dark—
With the way I speak,
The way I write,
The way I am.
Well, you see,
Life is painful,
And that is the bitter, honest truth.
I'm not going to act like everything is this
 wonderful journey
When I know it is not.
Sure, I can be happy,
And I can get joy out of simple daily pleasures,
But that's not going to hide the truth.
I'm not going to live a life full of lies,
I need the concrete, hard facts—
To live.

SIX

I thought that writing in purple pen would
>   make everything better.
I thought that all my problems would just vanish.
I thought that I would immediately become a
>   better writer.
I thought that I would drop 10 pounds and
>   become healthier.
I thought that I would become a happier person.
I thought that I would be unstoppable.
I thought that I could do anything.
I thought wrong.
For the color of a pen could fix my broken
>   dreams.
Silly me, nothing could ever do that—
Not even a purple pen.

SEVEN

I just think of when I used to hurt myself.
Now, I don't know why I did it.
I did it for pleasure,
For comfort—
Two things which no one gave me.
I did it because I deserved it,
For I was a screw-up—
One thing I was afraid to admit.
I did it to express my feelings,
For I had no other way to—
A complex idea that had ruined me.
But as much as I loved to do it,
I hated it.
I was scared,
A frightened child—
With no direction to go in.

COMPASS

Show me the way.
I'm weary and I'm afraid I can't go on.
Show me the way.
I'm anxious to be alone in this adventure.
Show me the way.
I've lost all sense of direction.
Show me the way.
North,
South,
East,
And West.
Show me the way out of this enigma that I call
    my mind.

EIGHT

Like a baby, I cry
Like a child, I sigh
Like an adult, I try
But sometimes, crying is selfish
And sighing is careless
And trying is worthless

NINE

There's this tree that I would visit when I was
        younger.
Its skinny trunk and its emerald leaves
Would glisten in the sun.
It gave me shelter when I was cold,
And a place to be alone.
There's this tree that I would visit when I was
        younger,
But it's gone now.
Its skinny trunk chopped down, and its emerald
        leaves just a memory.
I now have nowhere to go when I'm chilly,
And nowhere to be alone.

TEN

Think of me when you look at the sky—
The transition from warm magenta to deep
        indigo.
Think of me when you look at the stars—
Thousands and thousands of beautiful little
        lights.
Think of me when you look at the moon—
The illuminated crescent that puts you to bed.
Think of me.

ELEVEN

I like writing in pen.
It makes my handwriting look much neater,
And it makes me feel more official.
But the ink runs out with time,
And it will no longer write my feelings,
Or my stories,
Or my homework.
Nothing in life is timeless—
Especially the great things,
Like writing in pen.

TWELVE

Scribbles on paper are like clouds on a stormy
      evening,
Ready to erupt any moment.
Words on paper are like lightning on a warm
      summer night,
Illuminating the calm sky.
Sentences are like rain falling upon the rooftop,
Whispering stories in your ear.

THIRTEEN

A sliver turns into a cut,
A bump into a break,
A punch into a slash.
The days become shorter,
And the nights longer,
And the pain fuller.
But the cut becomes a scar,
The break begins to heal,
And the slash becomes a memory.
The days are now longer,
And the nights shorter,
And the pain limited.

LATE NIGHT SADNESS

I grab myself some fudge and a bottle of vodka
And plop myself on the couch.
I turn on some late-night television,
Listening to a story of a missing child.
Is that me? I think to myself.
I'm lost.
I gulp down another sip,
And lay my dreams to rest.
The suffering has become implanted within me,
And it won't ever go away.
Like a scar—
It is always there.
Like a memory—
To save for a rainy day.

PARANOIA

Footsteps echo in my mind,
Breathing off in the distance.

TUNNEL LOVE

In the tunnel I see a vision
Of you and me.

FOURTEEN

Mirrored—
The apparition of my face against yours.
Who is this stranger that I see in my reflection?
The ghostly, ivory-skinned woman?
The restless, lifeless ethereal being through this
        looking glass?
The limp, emaciated child that stands before me?
Mirrored—
The apparition of my face against my echo.

BLISTERING AFTERNOON

Whoosh, crackle, snap, roar
The green slowly turns to gray
Burning bright as hell

MUTE

. . . .

. .

. . . . .
. . . . . .

. . .
.

HONEYBEES & HONEYSUCKLES

The summer air whisks helicopter seeds
And juniper leaves scatter the garden.
The purple peonies emulate the ashen sky
And rush around waiting as I sigh.
All that's left are honeybees and honeysuckles,
Swarming in the air that I breathe.

FIFTEEN

Your flesh grabs my brittle arm,
And I know what's coming for me.

SIXTEEN

When I was an emotional wreck, you were
    always there.
But now you're no longer around for me.
Do I just lay here in my own pit of despair?
Wondering if you'll ever forgive me?
Because I need you—
Desperately.

SEVENTEEN

You'd whisper lullabies in my ear,
With your soft, sweet voice.
You'd trace my face with your fingertips,
Giving me the chills while being surrounded
       by your warmth.
You'd call me your princess,
When you were every nice word I could
       think of.

EIGHTEEN

A river flows through a broken creek,
Simple as my sorry life may seek.

NINETEEN

Answer the words that I do solemnly speak.

TWENTY

I was walking down the street at midnight in a storm. The rain pelted the pavement and embraced me in a calm shower. The streetlamps were foggy in the misty air. But I couldn't help notice one that was dimmer than the others. It had a slight flicker to it—as if it were hanging on to its last breath. And then I saw the boy. He was lying in the middle of the jagged road in his flannel pajamas. He couldn't have been more than the age of eight. Why was he up at this hour? More importantly, why was he lying face-down in the middle of the street in a storm? I wanted to ask him why—but then he disappeared. I blinked, and he was gone. He couldn't have gone very far, I thought. Rustling through the bushes and frantically chasing pavements led me into a deep depression. I'd lost the boy. He was in trouble. I could have helped him. I can still hear his sorrows echo off this dead end street and I know that he is out there and that he is frightened and scared and worried and alone. He is out there still. He must be lying face-down on another end of the road. But why can't I find him? How could I be so blind to what is really going on around me? I need to know where he is. I need to go find him. I need to know he is safe. I just need to know. I've gone mad. Looking for this boy who cannot seem to be found is making my head tick, tick, tick like a ticking bomb. My mind is on fire, and I start to brew up a fever. My lip quivers and my body starts to shake, but not from the chill of the rain. The shaking turns into convulsions and I no longer have control of my body. My heart rips out of my chest and my breaths linger in the sharp air and my mind starts to slow down, but it doesn't dissolve the pain. The boy's sickness is inside of me and I can't break free. It hits me full force, and my only option is to succumb to the depths. I'm not myself anymore. I'm not myself anymore. I am the boy. The boy in the flannel pajamas lying face-down in the pavement. The boy who was sobbing throughout the cold and broken storm. The boy who disappeared in just a matter of seconds. I am now face-down in the meager puddle written in the street. Is this where the sidewalk ends?

THE CREATION OF BIRDS

Inspired by Remedios Varo's 1957 painting,
Creation of the Birds

Mother Owl speaks a song,
Whispering sweet vibrations from her heart.
The moonlight grants life,
The shimmering skyline giving flight.
Mother Owl paints a picture,
Wisps of cerulean and silver from her brush.
The nighttime grants hope,
The little lights giving life.

TWENTY-ONE

I seem to have seen the seahorses swimming
softly in the sullen salty sea.

TWENTY-TWO

The whispers of the wind mask the solemn sounds of the sun.

TWENTY-THREE

The monster stirs inside my brain. Each waking day to each sullen night. I can't stop. I can't stop. The river creeps to my neck and suddenly I am under. I am masked by the plethora of H_2O molecules. I can't breathe. I can't breathe. Soon enough water fills my lungs and I can't breathe anymore. I can't breathe anymore. I can't…

TWENTY-FOUR

The moonlight casts my shadow behind me as I walk down the bare road. Something is stopping me from going any further. I should be heading back home so my mother won't worry about me like she always does.

I think I'm going to stay here a while. It's a nice night and who really cares if I'm a tad late home? I'll just explain the whole thing to my mother as soon as I arrive home. I can't get that bad of a punishment.

I push my chocolate brown hair out of my face and I prop myself on the cold pavement. I don't know what brought me to here, but I'm glad it did.

The wind blows my soft, silk hair back into my face. The breeze burns my charcoal gray eyes. It's getting kind of late, but I don't think I'm ready to leave yet.

The street lamp directly above me starts to flicker, then suddenly goes out. It's pitch black.

No other street lamps are on because on this street, they are motion-sensored, as I had now learned.

    I guess it would be better if I started my way home now.

TWENTY-FIVE

The bare back of the rider was hooked, pale. Violet and mahogany intertwined her scarred flesh. What could have caused this? The mile-wide smile of hers turns into a blue "O," realizing her struggle to breathe. The fluttering blue eyes of hers are now masked over by her ice-cold eyelids. Being in the cold left frost on her blue-black eyelashes. Her childhood has been taken from her, her youth, her innocence. It was hard to see her like this. Who did this? What did this? The rocking horse in the playground stares at me. The wind blows it slowly back and forth, leaving it squeaking softly in the cold, autumn day. Have you ever understood something that didn't seem real? My sister, left dead in the playground. Her cream shirt ripped off next to her. I feel her back, the rough scratches made my body shiver, mainly from fear. I've feared this day for my sister, finding me dead, but I never would have thought it the other way around. The slam of the tree in the distance makes me believe I know who did this. All that's left for me is to get my sister back and let this monster take me for who I am…

SPOKEN SILENCE

The sky paints the words that cannot be said
The rain repeats for all to hear

Though taken
Yet not understood
Leaves us helpless

For an answer we cannot find
Where the question is hidden beneath
The Silence

TWENTY-SIX

Take a rocketship to the moon,
Take a submarine out to sea

TWENTY-SEVEN

Think. Think. Think.
Time passes by. Hours upon hours. Days upon days. Weeks upon weeks.
We spend all our time thinking. And where does that bring us?
Thinking about everything.
Slowly killing us.

TWENTY-EIGHT

I never had a way with words. I could never create something beautiful by just talking or writing or thinking. It never came with ease. Intricately written lines that would never flow together, leaving everything incomplete. It just never worked out the way I wanted it to. I could sit for hours, wrapping my thoughts around my brain and onto the paper, but it never turned out right. And it never will turn out right. I'm just a person who cannot woo someone else with my words.

TWENTY-NINE

The monster inside your head
Holds dear to your heart
Smothers you silent

It's your best friend
And your worst enemy

It reaches down your throat
Strangling you,
But you're not dead
But you are dying

SHADOW

The darkness following me
Frightens me
Terrifies me
Yet I cannot escape it
Attached to my back
Dulling through the warm streetlights
I must rest in peace
But he will never leave
He is a part of me
And I am a part of him

THIRTY

Three o'clock in the morning
Time for biscuits and deep thoughts
For tea and reading classics
Noticing the little details
Each freckle, each yawn
Nothing can keep you quiet
But the thought of the approaching dawn

SUMMER LOVIN' HAD ME A BLAST

The crisp scones and the white trickle tree
Swarmed in the air above me
The lavender walls and the white picket fences
Wrapped me up without a tense
Summer lovin' had me a blast
Oh so fast

THIRTY-ONE

Why must we love the things we cannot have?

THIRTY-TWO

Because when the pages turn,
Everything moves on.
Because when the pages burn,
Everything is lost.

THIRTY-THREE

I love too hard and hold too tight.

THIRTY-FOUR

Show me love
Like the winter morning
Show me love
Like the summer breeze
Show me love

THIRTY-FIVE

It's not about the little room you hold, it's about the great room you despair.

THIRTY-SIX

What have I become?
Sculpted by you—
Sculpted by my fears—
Sculpted by the ice?
No.
Not anymore.
What I've become:
Sculpted by me—
Sculpted by my strengths—
Sculpted by the ground I walk on.

THIRTY-SEVEN

Ruptured by your flesh,
My heart skips a beat.
My heart skips another
And another.
My heart skips no longer.
Ruptured by your flesh,
My lungs skip a breath.
My lungs skip another
And another.
My lungs skip no longer.
But they also breathe no longer.
Ruptured by your flesh,
I am no longer.

THIRTY-EIGHT

Meanwhile I am waiting
Waiting for another way
Waiting for another day
Waiting for another say

VELVET KISSES

A fire ablaze,
A night of craze,
My love for you
Comes in waves.
A heart misses
Those velvet kisses,
My love for you
Comes in wishes.

THIRTY-NINE

For the sun to set, you must first let it go down.